Fears, Tears & Years of Dá Diva Jazz

Dá Diva Jazz

Fears, Tears & Years of Da'Diva

Copyright March 2018 By Jasmine Hampton
Published in the United States of America by
Harvest Wealth Publishing LLC 2018
An imprint of Harvest Wealth LLC

www.DaDivaJazz.com

Library of Congress Cataloguing-In-Publication Number
PENDING
ISBN 978-0-9843654-8-7
First Edition Printing
Printed in the United States of America
March 2018
Harvest Wealth Publishing LLC
200 Centennial Avenue Suite 200
Piscataway, NJ 08854

I dedicate this book to the women at Edna Mahan Correctional Facility, and all of those who continue to exist within the walls of the beast. I know the struggle and you are never forgotten.

ACKNOWLEDGEMENTS

First and foremost, I am giving honor to my Heavenly Father for saving my life and giving me a renewed life at a time when I wanted to end my life. No doubt, God You rock!

My parents, the late Sandra Lawrence aka my "Mama Faraha" and William Hampton aka "BaBa Malii," for riding with me whether I was wrong or right literally until their last breath. My maternal grandmother Gloria Harris, for all that you are and everything you have been to me all my life. You are the family rock and I love you to life.

To my sisters Camille and Stephina… God gave me the best when He blessed me with y'all. I know that I used to be a mess but I am thankful for the patience, love, support and no judgment along the way. Thank you for opening up your home and welcoming me back into the family when I came home.

To my other half, Khayree "Poparotsi" Wilkes. My first love at 11 years old. For God to send you back to me is a blessing I will never take for granted. I love you baby!

Nicole B. Simpson, there is much to be said about you lady! Not only are you my pastor and sister in Christ, but you are my rider. I thank you for being instrumental with my re-entry, for believing in me, and not judging me. I thank Harvest Wealth Publishing for bringing this book to life and sharing the vision with me.

To my diva, Rashida Smith, for having my back, being my diary and a true friend in a hopeless place. Thank you for your loyalty and your encouragement for me to keep on writing.

I want to acknowledge a few others who have been true to me along this journey with unconditional love, support & loyalty… My twin diva Nidrah Dixon- Lindsay, my sis & Dirts; Sharonda Patrick & Naseera Monk, my road dawg Bahiya Harris, my sister/friend Tiyanna Beckom, soul sista Nafeesa Goldsmith, my Aunties Sissie & Donna Mayo, my big sis Imani Malikini, former c/o Gangi, for motivating me to keep writing, believing in me and not being afraid to be an outcast among bad apples.

Dr. Michelle Tatar with the College of New Jersey and all the Wise Women connected with our "Women is the Word" group. Special shout out to Amare "Sup" Terrell (DTH Family) and my ZOO CREW family, specifically Hassan Harris, Altareek AKA Man-Man with Klutch Kutz & Alboo White for the welcome home love. No doubt, real people do real things!

Finally, to my queens still on lock in Edna Mahan Correctional Facility; Monique Kendall, Courtney Clement, Deborah Phillips, Lucretia Stone, Maria Montalvo, Nashali Gadson, Tawanna Murphy and so many others I may have forgotten to name. Charge it to my head and not my heart. Keep the faith, chin up & chest out…Salute!

INTRO

Within these pages are the innermost thoughts and emotions of an incarcerated mind. I am thankful that I have been a prolific writer because the only source of freedom for a diva to exist within the confines of this modern-day plantation is through the pen.

What you are about to encounter are more than mere words pressed on paper. It is entrance into the heart, mind and soul of the "Fears, Tears & Years" of Da'Diva. I first entered the prison system a young girl with an old soul yet refused to allow the circumstances of pain to define the very essence of my existence.

The following is a collection of poems written in chronological order throughout my transformation. I have decided to share my journey with all inquisitive minds curious about how one survives a long season of incarceration. From the moment those silver bracelets were slapped on my wrists I was stripped of everything! I was forced to live under conditions to which I am not accustomed, yet I realize I had made my bed.

Inside the four walls, freedom of speech is nonexistent. With the walls as ears to midnight cries, I managed to find my escape from this beast through my writing. You see, they may have my body but only I can give them my mind. Watching my words come to life on paper, I was free to travel to islands unknown to man, visit the past, alter the present and create the future… It's a beautiful thing y'all!

So for those who know me and been riding me to keep writing, consider this an appetizer to hold y'all off until the main dish is ready to be served. Smile 4 me baby and enjoy the read!

ONE,

Jazz

Young & Confused

(1995 Youth House Bid)

Young & confused is what I am

Living the street life

Not giving a damn

I'm always chillin and on the go

Getting my C.R.E.A.M.

In the cash flow

Now I'm locked down for a while

Doing my time killa style

I miss my boyfriend, family and friends

But it's all good

Cuz it ain't the end

I'm giving props to those who stood by my side

Those who didn't I ain't letting shit ride

So to all my peeps who know what I'm about

Coming straight from the Youthie

Here's a big shout out…

ONE LOVE

Me & My Boo-Boo

(1999 On the Run)

How happy you make me

While others disgrace me

You continue to date me

My fucked up thoughts keep me living in sin

But you give me strength within

Becuz you are a true friend

As I deal with trials & tribulations

Through our communication

I proceed with no hesitation

But these haters steady try'n to block my concentration

They fuckin wit my dome

Now I'm in a fuckin zone

All I want is my Boo-Boo to come home

Two years you been gone

Finger fuckin myself thinking of you it be on

Yo, I'm keeping it so real

These cornballs I don't feel

All I need is my Big Will

By my side

Before I catch a homicide

Cuz my fucked up mentality ain't letting shit ride

These mutts already trying to take me away

In ya arms I wanna lay

But Clinton is where they want me to stay

If these pigs wanna play

We could do the shit all day

Whether it's prison or the bricks I'm a always stay true

From now until eternity

It's Me & my Boo-Boo!

DIRT

(January 2000, On the Run)
I go through changes everyday
Tired of runnin these streets
Gotta find a better way
But all I can do is smoke and pray
Niggas is dying out here
I'm losing homies everyday
Out here stuck in a war zone
Knowing I need to take my ass home
Before some bitch ass nigga give me 1 to the dome
Nah, I ain't ready to die
But when I do that's when thugs cry
With bodies dropping back 2 back
Yea, that's how it multiplies
Snitch ass niggas come home with phony alibis
But Dirt a real bitch
I'll ride for mines
High as hell but shawty still a dime
Pretty face and smile plotting on my next crime
Sexing the mic gotcha nigga pressing rewind
And that bitch baby daddy keep me looking fine
So what I be hitting him on the celly
So he can fill my belly
With shrimp & spaghetti

And we stay at the telly
The bricks he be hitting me off
He copped me the car and the loft
Told me he like it soft
I don't even gotta suck his dick
Just tickle his balls
While I'm in the Lex
With the ice on my chest
Listening to Al Green comparing who sex is the best
Every time we apart I keep the bullet proof vest
Fuckin wit a hitter nigga, it's Dirt life til I rest!

Food 4 Thought

I fear loneliness, yet I crave solitude

Being separated from society

You learn not to trust everybody

Inmates become family

The walls are ears to midnight cries

Surrounded by pigs all day and night

"GET UP, SHUT UP, LOCK UP"

Life in the system is all corrupt

No justice

No peace

Just crooked ass police

They got hatred in they heart

And I got war on my mind

While these bitches steady playing

The medication line

Legal drugs are the worse

It's a jail house curse

They could keep that shit

Cuz I know my self-worth

"My people are destroyed from lack of knowledge

No knowledge of self

When are we going to free our minds

From being institutionalized??

Fallen Star

In the depths of solitude is where I stay

Concentrating and contemplating to find a better way

I'm surrounded by strangers who don't really care

My family is miles away

So how did I get here

I am alone

Without an ear to confide in

No one understands

The pain I hold within

I'm hurting, scared and all alone

I miss my sisters

And I want to go home

The tears from my eyes flow like rain

My life, my life

Will never be the same

Lord, I'm tired

How much longer must I be

A fallen star in this beast

Fighting to be free?

Your Eyes

Your eyes are mirrors to the soul

They were once calm & sweet

But now they've turned cold

Who caused this pain

That I see

Is it the world, yourself, or could it be me?

You say everything is cool

But the eyes never lie

Tell me what's wrong

Take off that disguise

Open up your soul and let me inside

I can feel your pain

Because yesterday I cried!

Confusion

What is it that I'm doing

I just don't understand

I'm crying out for guidance

Please dear Lord take my hand

My heart and mind says two different things

Which should I listen too

What does it all mean

My heart tells me to jump

My mind tells me not

What is going on

When will the confusion stop

I'm caught up in the meantime

While doing time

Searching for true love in between time

When will be the time

That I will truly know

Which one to listen too

And which one to let go?

I guess in the meantime I'll just let it flow

Which one is correct?

Only Lord knows…

21 Questions

What do you want from me?

For I have nothing to offer you

What do you see in me

For I am only 22

Why do you love me

When I can't fulfill your needs

Why do you want me

Answer me please!!

I am a victim in your world now

And at times I feel so lost

If you really love me then show me the way

Because to me you are the Boss

How can I please you? I just don't understand

I never been here before

So please be gentle with my hand

Your lips say forever

But your body screaming today

What road are we taking

Am I just in the way

What do you want from me???

Black Butterfly

Black Butterfly soaring high in the sky

Determined to reach the stars

Seen only from afar

Ambitious, intelligent and a lil conceited

To reach my goals

All of this is needed

Although in the past I have been mistreated

I won't give up until my mission is completed

Black Butterfly, how beautiful the sight

In the midst of the storm

You continue to fight

So delicate, tender, sweet yet sour

Deep within self you have the power

To take control in this war

Keep shining, stay focused and continue to soar

Black Butterfly

4 Give Me

Never meant to hurt you
Never wanted to see you cry
Never wanted to feel this pain
That we feel inside
As the night turns to dawn and a new day begins
All I can say is "I'm sorry"
Over and over again
Sometimes I wonder if things will ever be the same
A love so pure
Has been invaded with pain
How can I ease the pain and get you back again
If I could, I would
But it's like a no win
All I know is that I love you
Til death do us part
Please, forgive me for my deception
And mend your fragile heart.

Smile

Sometimes it amazes me

How much strength one can find within self

It's like in the midst of these trials and tests I manage to

smile

Even when I really want to cry

I mask the hurt and pain of the past AND present behind this

warm heart as I continue to keep hope alive

These mesmerizing eyes have seen too much to go back

And at times too much to go on

But still I smile

I smile becuz I'm happy

I smile becuz I'm sad

I smile becuz I can remember

All of the good times I've had

I smile becuz I am loved

I smile becuz I can love

I smile becuz I love myself

I smile becuz the enemy is laughing

I smile becuz he won't laugh long

I smile becuz I am a mom

I smile becuz I am a daughter, sister, lover and friend

I smile becuz if I didn't then I wouldn't be Jazz

I smile becuz the world can just kiss my ass

So smile 4 me baby!

I AM

I AM an Ebony Queen robbed of my innocence and freedom

So do not insult my character by thinking of me as just

another young girl with a fat ass and pretty face

For my beauty shines through the stillness of the night

And my brilliance will blind all who enters my circumference

I am the foundation to the conception of love

I've come in peace

Yet you're trying to tear me in pieces

Why?

Is it becuz you fear my courageous ways and determination

to achieve and succeed

Or is it the way I so easily adapt to my surroundings

While refusing to become a product of my environment

I have conquered my weakness in this battle for freedom

For when I was weak God made me strong

Every day I awake in this hell and continue to press on

I am a Kings kid and will continue to shine

Becuz I know that all things are possible

With God on my side

Unbelievable

Sitting on a mission so pay attention

You brought Da'Diva out of me

So fuck the competition

It's not my destiny to be lonely

I could hook up with these groupies who be on me

But they phony

With you it's different

I got no need to be suspicious

Cuz I just know

My life with you would be delicious

From the moment we met

I must admit I was playing for keeps

Damn, can't help but wait

To take this to the streets

Aint bout no fuckin and suckin but it plays a part

Stevie Wonder could see that you got my heart

I wanna kiss you in places I ain't never been

If I could I would

But our situation is a no-win

Wish we could sit back and kick it

The power in those chinks really got me addicted

I'm ready to say "fuck it" and go all out

Run up in ya space and let you see what I'm about

Throw Peaches in ya mouth

And give me 5 minutes
Not even that
Cuz Money stroke is strong and my clit is fat
Knowing these bitches they done told the fuckin cops
Pigs runnin in Stowe ready to take a bitch to lock
But I ain't giving up til my mission is completed
To give you good loving
I'll do whatever needed
I want to give you happiness and maybe even more
I told you before
No time to waste just giving what you're looking for
I swear sometimes this place makes me bitter
But I won't give up
Cuz I never was a quitter
You're giving me lovin and keep me on my toes
I respect you to the fullest
And this everyone knows
Whoever would have thought that I'd find this love in jail
Where this is going
Only time will tell
I know that I'm not giving up
Cuz baby you a keeper
Through all this madness
Our love is getting deeper
Incredible
Unstoppable

Your love is wonderful

As the world turns we continue to grow

Our love is stronger than Tyson

More precious than gold

I'll go through hell and back

For our story to be told

Where did you come from

How could this be

It's like God knew what I wanted

And made you a reality

Sometimes I think you're too good for me

Cuz all I ever felt was hurt

You switched me up

And brought Da'Diva out of Dirt

I respect that

Never regret that

By ya side

Is always where I'm at

Never giving up

And I'm never letting go

You saw wifey

When them niggas saw hoe

I ain't lying just letting it flow

This love I found is

Unbelievable!

Another Sleepless Night

Another sleepless night
Another fucked up day
When will this pain
Just go away
So much drama in my life
So many tears that I shed
So many times I wish
That I could be somewhere else instead
Is it the color of my skin
That makes things so bad
Or this life filled with sin
That keeps me so sad
Another sleepless night
And I don't know why
Another sleepless night
That all I do is cry
Another sleepless night
That I crave to be held
To feel the comfort of real love
Instead of this pain spell
My blessings have now become a curse
I am 22 years young
Feeling nothing but hurt
Another sleepless fuckin night!!!!!

Crooked

At night I can't sleep

Steady tossin & turnin

Thinking bout this lesson that I'm learning

Everyday is a struggle

And it's driving me crazy

Sometimes I wish I was dead

With my brother and my baby

This world that we live in is all corrupt

We got mama's killing babies

Straight not giving a fuck

Niggas on the corners trying to earn a fast buck

And if you wear the wrong colors

They'll light ya ass up

It's a new millenium and the game done changed

Got cops more crooked than me

And they say I'm strange?

They done labeled me a menace to this fucked up society

Got me ready to start blacking

In all type varieties

But I'm a hold my head

And maintain the pressure

Being a warrior in this beast

These pigs try to test ya

Only peace I got

Is the peace within
My notebooks my world
And my pen is my best friend
I write in the dark
Becuz the light hurts my eyes
Everyday a crooked smile
Be my only disguise
This pain in my heart
When will it end?
Wish I can turn back time
And start all over again
I'll go back to when I was a little kid
Correct the things I did
To stop myself from doing a bid
But right now Mommy can't help me
And homies don't know me
I'm surrounded by bitches
And the meds can't control me
These low budget bitches is so fuckin phony
Trying to be my friend
But they aint even a friend to they self
Sorry ass bitches are bad for my health
I could spit all day
About these geeks and freaks
Compared to me
All of these lames is weak

Life through my eyes will scare they ass to death

Poverty, murda, violence

And never a moment to rest!

Hey God

Hey God, I feel stranded
And I don't know why
I'm ready to spread my wings
But all I can do is cry
At times I can't help but to wonder why
You gave me a prince
And then you let him die
You let my baby daddy whoop my ass
And introduce me to the streets
At the age of 15
Out there tryin to eat
Sex, drugs and violence
There was never any rest
At times I begged you
To take my last breath
Moms said it was a test
And til this day I don't understand
Why I was born a Queen
Yet forced to be a man
On the block with my homies
Straight ballin with the heat
Looking over my shoulder
For them cats we robbed last week
I was even homeless

Though I denied it to myself
Every other day laying my head
Somewhere else
Fuckin mad niggas
Though bad for my health
I was in it for survival
And not for the wealth
Lord you sat back and let all this be
Yet they say you got love for me?
You let drugs intervene and rip my fam apart
Mom dukes got addicted
Gramma got a broken heart
I begged you for years to let moms be free
And now that she is
You gave her HIV?
Lord, I just don't understand
All of the pain one must bare
Wish you give me a sign
That you're listening up there
If this is so then answer my prayer
I just really need to know
That someone really cares
Lord, I need you
To show me the way
And if you can't stop the pain
Then take me today…

Hey God

(Part II, 3 Years In)
Hey God, shit is hard!
I'm sitting in a prison yard
On my way to trial
With a new charge
I'm trying to deal with this shit
Cuz this shit can't be it
A young diva with no name
Only 6 digits
Yo life is crazy
But I'm living it up
Surrounded by pigs
Still not giving a fuck
Getting mad fan mail
From cats I don't know
Either read about me in the papers
Or heard I was a hoe
Nah, I aint a hoe
Just about the dough
But dough aint shit
When you facing death row
Yo G, what the fuck
Can you feel my pain
I'm in sweats and khaki's

Instead of Armani X-change

I saw better days

But now that has changed

The sun don't shine no more

All it do is rain

I'm finger fuckin in rec

To relieve some stress

Chics wit dicks

Yo, my life is a mess

I'm trying my best

But I need some goods in my chest

Late night on my knees

It's to you I confess

This life filled with sin & tragedy

My mental capacity

Goes beyond this shit

So yo, it gotta be

Another way to get out this bitch

Sitting in this cell I lose consciousness

Living with fiends and non-descript's

Getting head in the closet

Yo this can't be it!

Hey God if you love me

Then don't say fuck me

Love me or leave me

But I prefer that you love me

I did a lot of things

And my ways was real ugly

Poisoning my body

Just to feel lovely

Indeed I came a long way

And got a ways to go

Lookin for love

Where it's at?

I don't know

Man, shit got me stressing

I'm sick of confessing

I got a hit on the D.A.

So you tell me if I learned my lesson

I'm tired

I'm lonely

I'm fuckin hurt

Maybe I won't feel this pain

Once I'm in the dirt

Yeah, that's right

It's my time to go

But before I do

I'm letting you know

I loved everything in this world

More than myself

So now it's time

For me to love something else:

BOOM!

I just killed myself…

HEY GOD

Shit

I tried to warn you in the beginning

That I had a lot of shit with me

But you chose to ignore it

And made me wifey

Years later a lot has changed

Most of the shit is gone

But it has left a stain

The stench from the shit

Is starting to push you away

I can't bare to let this be

So I'm cleaning it today!

Black Butterfly

(Part 2)

A Black Butterfly with a broken wing

How can she fly

Can she do anything

She's so sweet yet bitter

As she watches the other butterflies fly

They're not as talented as she

They can only soar but so high

But the Black Butterfly

With all of her skills and beauty

Can reach the stars

If only given the opportunity

But who will help her

Who will stop that long

To mend her wing

So that she can move on

Or will they all be vindictive and keep flying away

To keep her down

While they all go play

Black Butterfly

Girl, dry those tears

For your wing isn't broken

It's been healed for years

Emotional Rollercoaster

Up & down
Round & round we go
On the emotional rollercoaster
One never knows
When will it stop or start
It's a ride too risky
For a fragile heart
In & out of my life
You came and went
And now that you're gone again
I can't help but to reminisce on the times we've spent
Indeed we had our issues
But we always worked them out
I can't even front
That at times I had my doubts
"Real love conquers all"
Are the words that we live by
And now that you're gone again
I can't even cry
I guess I'm now used to this ride
After so many years
Maybe when the ride is over
I'll shed my final tears…

Good Bye

(4 Bahiya)

We had good times and bad

Both happy & sad

But no matter what

We always had each other backs

We experienced a lot throughout the years

Seducing ballers, getting money and high with our peers

When our peeps passed away

We both shed tears

Got fucked up and represented pouring out a lil liquor

Through all the pain

Our bond grew thicker

Remember how we vowed that we were "dawg's til the end"?

Well, the end must be now

Becuz I can't find my friend

I guess that it's not a bad thing though

Becuz times have changed

You got a baby girl now

And me?

I'm just trying to maintain

Ain't no love lost

Cuz dawg you my heart

It just hurt so bad

Knowing the game done tore us apart

You'll always have a friend in me

As I have in you

But now it's time for us to let go

And finally face the truth

No more hustling, living reckless, or getting high

So to those in my past

I must say goodbye

Sorry yall, I just can't take it no more

I done rode for so long

It's time to do it raw

So stay doing you

Like we always do and did

While I continue holding it down

Doing this bid…

Good Bye!

Amazing Love

I see forever in your eyes

And damn those chinks got me hypnotized

Although I've tried to fight it

I can no longer deny

That I think I'm going to love you

Until the day I die

To front is to lie

To lie is to be fake

I know this is something you despise

And truly hate

You are here for me

Through these difficult times

And baby I swear it feels as if

I'm losing my mind

But you give me so much strength

Without much fuss

I finally realize

That the truth is us

Damn, it's so amazing to be loved!

They Don't Know

I'm up in this mutha zoned out

On some other shit

But they don't feel me though

Although my presence is felt

As I continue to exist within the depths of solitude

How can they understand someone so authentic, intricate,

audacious yet intimate?

Can they see the blood in my eyes and the ammunition in

my heart?

To see past this ebony skin, pretty face and smile

The meekness in my voice and the sway of my hips

As I continue to stride

With my head held high

Definitely the calm before the storm!

Do they know

Or are they afraid

To face the wrath of Da'Diva

To dig deeper into the core of my being

With all the abuse, neglect, frustrations and beatings

As I recognized the snakes

Keep the fakes in they place

And cuss death face to face

Hell no

They don't really know

And damn sure aint ready
So for that I am
And will remain
The last of a dying breed!

Unfaithful

You hit me, so I hit you

You hit me back

And left a bruise

Tit for tat

Back to back

Up & down we go

The love that was once so strong

Is now fading with each blow

Why must you be unfaithful

Why must you do me wrong

How can you say that you love me

When you've hurt me for so long

I'm so sick of this shit

I've had enough

And now I'm out

You can keep your hoes now

Becuz a sucka is not what I'm about!

Realness

(4 Those in My Past & Those Curious)
A big heart with an old soul
Realness is my only crime
Yet all of those I gave myself too
Are the ones I cannot find
They lied, deceived, stole and hate
When I spoke the truth
Loved with no limits
And went out of my way
They said that they loved me
When shit was all good
But once temperatures rose
And times got hard
My loyalty was misunderstood
I asked myself over & over
"What did I do so wrong"
Though I count a lot of mistakes
The truth is I just didn't belong
For the devil is a liar
And God is truth
One can't serve two masters
That's why my friendship was abused
Yet still I am
The realest of them all
And my realness will remain standing
While those around me fall

I Love U

For all that you are
And all that you do
For being here for me
And remaining true
I love u
For wiping away my tears
Putting up with my bullshit
All throughout the years
Bringing laughter into my life
And calming my fears
I love u
For just being you and allowing me to be myself
For accepting my faults
With no comparison to somebody else
For pulling me out of darkness
And showing me the light
Giving me strength
When I thought I couldn't fight
I love u
Baby, you mean the world to me
Mere words can't begin to express
And although I despise this situation
Meeting you I don't regret
I love u!

The One

A true woman is secure with her emotions and confident in her looks

Truly a precious gem for you to obtain

Her wisdom is forever

Just as love lives with its lover

Though all her wisdom was learned through pain

A true woman

She's the One

You may ask who?

But the question is "who do you want her to be"?

She can be the one who gives life to a lonely soul

Or the teacher who causes the blind to see

She can be your mentor to pain

If you cross her with game

But this is something

That she chooses to disdain

She's much rather be your friend, wife, your lover and mother

Just as clouds flow under the sun

Once again I must remind you

That love lives inside her

Screaming out to you that

"She's The One"

Love

What of a love
That's unspoken of
As the sun kisses your face
And the wind gives you a hug
Everyday you awake
It touches your heart
And puts a smile on your face
It calms your fears
Dries your tears
A love so faithful
For all of these years
It doesn't envy, deceive, lie or cheat
It lifts your spirits
And gives strength when you're weak
This beautiful love
That I'm speaking of
Is not in human form
But comes from above
Lord, I'm so grateful
I don't know what to do
All I can say is that
"I love you" too
Thank you Jesus!

Gramma

I saw the tears in ya eyes
Yesterday on the v.i.
As you took a look around
With the cops in our b.i.
You can't really touch me or hold me
Grab me or console me
You're so used to being the boss
But now the pigs try to control me
You tell me "baby it's gonna be okay"
As you silently pray
For our strength and a better way
You feel my pain
And Lord knows I wish you didn't
As you blink the tears away
All you say is "it was written"
You always warned me about the snakes
But now that I've been bitten
I'm still fighting through the venom
And I'm never quitting
I thank the Lord up above
For having you in my life
I did a lot of wrong
But for you I'll do right
My only wish is to someday make you proud

To put a smile on ya face
As you say "that's my grandchild"
As of right now, it's only a dream
But this dream will come true
As long as you're on my team
So please Gramma
Just hold on and have faith
You mean the world to me
And no one can ever take your place
I look forward to the day
When we can laugh face to face
Without the pigs on our backs
As I yearn your tender embrace
But don't worry about me Cuz I'm gonna be alright
Struggle is in my blood
So everyday is a fight
I made a lot of mistakes
But this one I won't repeat twice
I'm getting closer to God
And just trying to keep my mind right
As I feed my dome
And stay focused through these lessons
I've learned to stop counting my losses
And be thankful for my blessings
A blessing you are
My angel in disguise

My prayer partner, my heart, the apple of my eye

At times I wanna give up

But for you I will try

To be all that I can be

Until the day I die

We're gonna be alright Gramma

And make it through these tests

As I vow to be the best

Til my last breath

And always remember

I love you beyond death

Numb

Thought I was numb
That I couldn't feel any more
But the pain is so real
As the tears continue to pour
I try to be strong
Try to do what's right
As I hold my head
And continue to fight
But as the years pass on
The pain only grows
There's a hole in my heart
That no one knows
Or maybe they do
And just don't care
Do they know where I've been
And how I really got here
All of my life all I wanted was peace
I searched for it in many ways
That has only brought me grief
But now, perhaps the numbness of pain
Will grant me thy release

Melting Clocks

I'm up and can't sleep

Got a lot on my mind

Melting clocks, melting clocks

Like I'm runnin out of time

Runnin out

Runnin too

Or away I don't know

The clock is ticking

And yet, I still can't let go

Melting clocks are what I see

When I close my eyes

Sex, murda, drugs

And hungry children cries

Dudes yelling "One time"

As the cops roll by

And a grieving mother screaming

She don't want her baby to die!

Melting clocks still melting

As the world moves on

Every minute on the hour

A new baby is born

Will they even make it

To see what's next

In this world filled with tragedy

And terroristic threats
It's like we're melting away
And only I can see it
Melting clocks
Melting clocks
You better believe it!

Love is Pain

It's an awful feeling to be in love
And away from your peeps
I mean, you crave them in ways
That are all too deep
Every couple that you see
And love song you hear
Reminds you of your baby
And how you wish they were near
You toss and turn
All through the night
Craving that special someone
To just hold you tight
Lack of sleep
Can barely eat
And when we do speak
My insides get weak
Damn, I'm in love
And sometimes I hate it!
I am missing my baby
And I can't even fake it
It's a bitter/sweet feeling
And I'm trying to shake it
Man, being in love
Will drive you insane
I guess I now know that
Love is Pain!

I Hate U

I hate u

For raping my people

Making and breaking ya own laws

And yet, you call us equal

I hate u

For riding through our hood

And looking down on our kids

Becuz the ghetto is where they live

And they parents doing bids

I hate u

So much right now

For coming for my crown

Trying to make bow down

Yo, that's funny

Bow down?

To who?

U?

Man, fuck u!

U make me sick

Smelling like a wet dogs dick

Coming for me

Right in ya face I'm a spit

I hate u bitch!

U and ya KKK clique

Wish I had the ratchet

Sit on the roof

And all of yall will catch it

Straight empty the banana clip in ya ass

With the quickness

Cuz I'm bitter, numb, full of hate and vengeance

I'll sew ya ass cheeks together

While you steady repenting

Oh, so now you want to pray?

God won't help you baby

Cuz it was you

Who put my peoples in slavery

Oh, I thought you was so brave

Now you crying and begging

For me not to put you in the grave

Fuckin Wood

U my slave!

I'll tie you up to the fence

While you repent

And fuck you in the ass with a hot stove iron

Oooh, now you crying

Shiit, just think about all the tears my mama shed

Before she went to bed

And how ya son shot my brother

With one to the head

If you think I got mercy for ya kind think again

U fuckin with a crazy black bitch

Who will DIE before I let you win

And right here

Right now

Is where I begin

POWER 2 THE PEOPLE!!!!

Jailing

I've experienced a lot of heartache and bull shit in the past

Yet, here you are

Claiming that this love will last

What makes you so sure

That I'm really the one you've search for

Is it my beauty or the booty

Or becuz I'm hard-core

Or is it all game

To help pass ya time

Are you just jailing off of me

Playing games with my mind

Until you are free

Back in the world and forget about me

How do I really know if you are true

Only time

Will tell the truth

But if only you knew

My nigga

I'm jailing off you too

Fuck I look like Boo!

Birth

July 30th, 1996
A friend drove me to the hospital
Becuz I was feeling sick
Seventeen years young
And 6 months pregnant with child
I sat in the cold waiting room
For a while
As I filled out papers
The staff treated me as a joke
But then as I vomited
My water suddenly broke
Panic, hysteria and fear plagued my mind
All I could say was:
"It's not time, it's not time"
Now as I lay in the hospital bed
All type of emotions
Are flowing through my head
With doctors and nurses talking around me
As if I was not there
A scared, lonely woman-child I was
But shit, I'm laying right here
Not to mention the contractions
Flowing through my spine
I spit on the nurse, cussed and screamed

As though I was losing my mind

Well, I guess the staff had enough

Becuz they filled my I.V. with drugs

So I could shut up

Temporarily sedated

The pain was gone

But @ 6:58am it was back on…

"That stupid ass nurse

Thought she was so slick

I got something for her

Right in this bed I'm a shit"

I took a deep breath

And pushed hard is hell

Then from between my legs

I heard a big wail

"Doctor, doctor, come quick and help me please"

What I thought was my bowels

Turned out to be my seed

Indeed, I gave birth

To an angel in disguise

Words could never express what I felt

The first time I looked into his eyes

"Karon Thomas Lewis"

Is the name of my prince

He passed 3 days later

And I haven't been the same since

One pound 3 ounces

Is what my baby weighed

He was too good for this world

And so God took him away

And now my child is out there

Somewhere in the heavens above

Patiently waiting for Mommy & Daddy

To bless him with our love…

I love you son!

Whispers In The Wind

What is it that you are saying to me

Is it for me to understand and see

I hear Your voice

So soft in the wind

Giving me guidance

But I don't know where to begin

You tell me:

"Be still"

But I run

You tell me to "speak"

Yet, I hold my tongue

You even send the birds to sing

My Lord, please tell me

What does it all mean?

I asked You for comfort

And You sent Your Holy Spirit

The Wind whispers all the time

But I refuse to hear it

I Cried

Last night I cried

And it made me feel sooo good inside

I cried for the past, present and the unknown

I cried for those suffering, lost

And my homies that's gone

Then as memories flowed

Through my head

I cried even more

Becuz I could be dead

In a way the tears

Were a sense of release

So tonight I cry

Becuz God has given me peace

Gotta Go

It's time to let go

Time to move on

You can't hold onto something or someone

Who is too far gone

Nor can you save the world

Or force them to change

All of that is only adding

Unnecessary stress on the brain

It's time to let go

Time for to say goodbye

Indeed I love you

But not enough to die

Our love is wrong

And we can't make it right

I've survived many wars

But with God

I can't fight…

I gotta go!

Senses

Smell?

I can't smell

For the walls are closing in

I'm claustrophobic

Trapped in this beast

And I don't know where to begin…

Smell?

My nose is stuffy

Eyes bloodshot red

I'm now numb to the pain

And my senses like a corpse

Are dead

I'm beyond frustration

For even that fragrance has passed me by

The walls are closing in

Loneliness is my only friend

Yet, it's the scent

Of a pigs fate

That gets me high

Tell Me Why

(1992, For My First Fallen Friend Tabu H. Reese)

Tell me why

Tell me, oh tell me

Why did you have to die

Now that you gone

I cry every night

Wishing that you were here

To hold up the fight

I wish you were here

So that I can say

That you were special

In so many ways

At your casket

I hold my breath

Repeating over and over

Just how I hate death

You were only here for a while

But you always knew

Just how to make me smile

Your voice and laughter

Stays in my head

As I close my eyes

I just know you're not dead!

Tell Me Why Part 2

(2006)

Just tell me why

My peoples had to fight for so long

Why I'm sitting in a cell

And my real homies long gone

Why my so call peoples

Got blocks on they phones

Why I ride for the hood

But now I'm alone

Why did the cops kill my brother

They put a hit on my lover

And my best friend sister

Sold me out to an undercover

Tell me why?

Why I love so hard

And always get my feelings hurt

Why my peeps laying the dirt

For putting in that work

Why dat clown ass nigga took my pussy

When I said no

He beat me up

And called me a hoe

Why I never pressed charges

But kept it to myself

Why he give me chlamydia

And jeopardized my health

Tell me why yo!

Hunger

It's color is black as the snake pit
That I'm forced to live in
It's color is the cold hard lump of nothing
That exists in the midst of confusion
It's the waiting on visits
That never show
The blocks on the phones
And the once beautiful glow
Of my sheroe
Hunger...
It's the blackness in the pupils
Of a hard turned cold
The sound of gunshots
That pierces a grieving mothers soul
Hunger is the color of emptiness
In the bowels of third world children
It's the hand me down sneakers
On a fatherless childs feet
The color of crack heads
As they walk the streets
Hunger...
It's the sound of the gavel
Hitting the bench
As the judge gives you jail time

That just doesn't make sense
Hunger is wanting so badly to be free
To preserve your soul
While not losing your dignity
Hunger is keeping pictures of your enemies
Visualizing them all in a casket
It's giving birth to a baby
Who is labeled as a bastard
Hunger is being born BLACK
In this world full of shit
Hunger is a being a warrior in this bitch
And this I'll never forget
Damn, I'm Hungry!!!

If I Could

(For MeMe & Steph)

If I could I would protect you from all of the ugliness in the
world

Fake smiles, lies, jealousy, envy, hate

Violence, drugs, poverty and perverts

Who try to manipulate

If I could

I would fight all of your battles

Weather every storm

Climb any mountain and cross any sea

This I'd gladly do

Just to protect your purity

Lord knows that I would

If only I could

Unfortunately, life doesn't rock like that

For we all have our own lessons to learn

Yet, I will always warn you about the snakes

And show you the rocks they're under

To keep you from being bitten

This I would

Becuz I could!

Love Jones

I can now understand why Van Gogh

Cut off his ear

For love, in its truest form is beautiful but frustrating

When that person isn't near

You think about them

In every love song you hear

And couple that you see

Anticipating and forever waiting

For you to come back to me

Oh, it's been so long

Since I have touched my baby

Fourteen months and six days

And it's driving me crazy

But I don't want the haters

To see me cry

So I shut down

And stay occupied

But deep down inside

My heart is aching

If you listen close enough

I'm sure you can hear it breaking

For true love is never faking

Or mistaking

But I do my best

To send my love to you

Through words pressed on paper

Sealed with a kiss

And sent to you

But it never seems to be enough

Becuz I still crave your tender touch

Damn, I miss you so much

I'm about to go nutts

Baby, if you're reading this

Then feel me please

Just close your eyes, listen to your heart

And then you will see

That our love is forever standing

And you're all that I need…

Frustrated

I wanna fuck you

But you're not here

When I put you out my mind

You seem to reappear

Oh how I crave just to have you near

As you caress my breasts

And nibble on my ear

I wanna fuck you

Just to feel your tongue against my flesh

Panting and moaning

"Daddy you are the best"

As I explode in your mouth until there's nothing left

I wanna fuck you

In ways I didn't know

Cowgirl style and upside down

With my head to the floor

You're digging in my gutts

As I beg for more

You then flip me over

And enter my back door

Now as I feel apart of you inside of me

I'm throwing it back

Oh so professionally

Damn, you're my baby and it feels so good

To stay in this position forever

I wish we could

I wanna fuck you

Until the crack of dawn

The % yells

"Count time"

I open my eyes and now you are gone

Tears of frustration surface

Becuz with you is where I belong

I can't even nutt in my dreams

Now you know that's just wrong…

Inspiration

(For Gangi)

You inspire me to birth my blessings out of a curse

As I maintain my sanity through the worse

I mean…

You don't speak as I do

Yet, you understand my talk

You haven't seen or been where I have

But you understand my walk

You inspire me to follow my dreams

And make them a reality

As you ignore the labels

Placed on me by society

You called me a "woman"

In its truest sense

This I already know

But coming from you

I can't express just how much it meant

There are no hidden agendas

As I press this pen

I just wanted to say

"Thank you"

And that I consider you a friend

Broken Glass

(Dedicated to Stratford Place)

Broken glass
Where little girls play double dutch and hopscotch
With little patches of grass here and there
Bicycles
Firecrackers
Little boys throwing rocks
And picking with the girls jumping rope
The Milk Bar
With one dollar shot glasses
Some drunk lady dances
And the big boys on the corner slang dope
Green Acres park with 1 set of monkey bars
Playing "catch a girl get a girl"
Ya knees get scarred
Gramma growing greys
Frying fish fillets
With sugar free Kool-Aid
To drink during the day
Damn, I wish we could've stayed
On the lookout for stolen cars
June Bug smiling
Gold teeth with stars

Jherri curls dripping

Flat tops with parts

Fellas free styling in ciphers

To see who got the most bars

Jelly shoes

Pink & Blue

Chillin on the roof

Throwing water balloons

Man, on the Rock

The things we do

Mama in finger waves

Every Friday night playing spades

Plus she even heard

That Lil Rah-Rah was gay

No pain

Waking up to piss stains

Heard my neighbor down the hall

Let them dudes run a train

Damn, how I miss those things!

Fire hydrants soak and wet

Moms getting into fights

Cuz her kids she gotta protect

It seems a bit dysfunctional

But it's home on Bedrock set!

Yesterday I Thought of Her

Sand & Sable perfume

Mixed with the scent of Newports and Gin

Eyes bloodshot red, black & blue

Hidden behind snake skinned Gazelles

Lips lined to perfection

Linen suits

Enzo shoes

MGM bag

With colored money stashed

Head held down

With two kids in hand

They look up at their Earth

She looks down

Not at her seeds

But at the ground

The rent is due

She sings the blues

Can have any man she choose

But she chose

Him…

Yesterday I thought of her

When Your Heart Turns Cold

When your heart turns cold

The love that was growing

Has ceased to unfold

Now as you look into her eyes

Another story is told

Is this the same woman

You used to kiss and hold

And that's how it is

When your heart turns cold…

You don't know who she is anymore

She used to be your world

Now she's just another girl

All the hops and dreams

Of what might be

Has now exploded to face reality

All you ever wanted was to be her lover

But now you're disappointed

And disappointment is a muthafucka

How could she do this?

Why did she wait so long?

It's been 5 years for nothing

And now you no longer belong

No existence

Or even the faint sound of love

Your heart is now cold

And no one can warm it

Except for God above..

I know that I hurt you

And now I must live with the guilt

But my love is still standing

On the foundation that was built

I'm so sorry baby

I wish that I could just press rewind

Take it back to yesterday

When I was yours and you were mines

I don't know how to fix this

But it's worth a try

Becuz I just can't bring myself

To let go or say good-bye

Right now your heart is so cold

And I don't know what to do

I just pray that you'll forgive me

And know that I will always be here for you!

Death

When will it stop

When will it end

When will my world

Come together again

My life has been put on hold

Somebody please tell me

When will I regain control

The days are gloomy

And it rains all the time

The nights are pitch black

And the stars don't shine

The birds don't sing

And the wind doesn't blow

The sun doesn't shine

And the flowers don't grow

I'm dying

I feel it

The end is near

After so much pain

I'm ready to face my biggest fear

Tell Gramma I love her

And kiss my sisters good-bye

It's time for me to go now

And I can't even cry

I done fought for so long

That I have nothing left

The fight is now over

Here comes my last breath

That's what it is

When you're surrounded by death!

HIM

He's a teacher

He's a preacher

A doctor

A poet

He's a brother

A husband

A father

Did you know it

He has seen many moons

In this lifetime

Fought for the rights

Of both yours and mines

Now he may have his head held down

But don't you dare

Turn up your nose and frown

He doesn't bother anyone

As they pass by

Hidden tears in his eyes

Yet, he can't even cry

Indeed this man has paid his debt

Homeless or not

Give "Him" some respect!

Someday

Someday I hope to see the world

And touch the hearts

Of every boy and girl

To become the woman

I was created to be

Live my life for the Lord

Becuz He cares for me

Someday I want to be a mom, wife, lover & friend

For the pain to cease

And happiness begin

For laughter and smiles

To replace the tears & heartache of the past

To walk out of these gates

And scream: "FREE AT LAST"

Someday I want to be a writer

Let the world see how much I'm a fighter

To tell my story

Of how hard it's been

Living in a cell

When I was born a Queen

Someday.. Someday… Someday

Until that day comes

I continue to exist within the war in my mind

Loneliness is your only friend

When you're doing time
As I sit here calculating all these years I've fought
I have to believe that someday my existence
Will be more than just a thought

4Ever

I cannot stay in here 4ever

I have so much to do

I cannot stay in here 4ever

My life isn't through

If I were to see 4ever

This is surely not the place

I cannot stay in here 4ever

Only a number with a face

I've set goals in life

All I want now is success

I cannot stay in here 4ever

For 4ever

Will be death!

Who Am I?

I Am She

Who made He

Unto thee

Come to be

Through dry birth pains

Did I labor in vain

For even the stars in the sky

Spell out my name

And you ask

Who am I?

Who are you?

For it was I and my tribe

Who made it through

I didn't get sick in the passage

Or throw myself overboard

In fear of the masters

And my son?

He aint a black bastard

I'm not your sambo, mammie, cum dumpster or bitch

I'm the sista on the front lines

Throwing up a closed fist

I wear my crown with pride

With my king by my side

But you throw on a white sheet

As your coward disguise

AmeriKKKa

So call home of the brave

Well if you so brave

Then how about you be my slave!

Here We Go Again

Damn, I just can't win

That Puta called love

Has hurt me again

I tried to hold on

Tried to make it right

But it's hard to do

When you're steady putting up a fight

My gloves are still on

And I'm ready for another round

Or did you think that I'll just let you go

Without a faint whisper or sound?

No doubt, I can't force you to be here for me

But I can show you exactly

Where I want to be

In hopes that you'll abandon your doubts

Look into your heart and see

That I belong to you

And you with me

I'm not kicking backs

Becuz that's certainly not my style

But do you think that she'll stay true

After a while

I know for a fact

That she can't love you like I do

But I guess that I'll let you see for yourself
While I remain true to only you
The pain inside is all too real
My heart is breaking into pieces
So much so that I can't even feel...
Here we go again!

Mentally I'm Free

Mentally I'm free

Surrounded by love, peace and purity

The very essence of beauty

In it's truest form

No longer within the depths of solitude

But at last

"Da Diva" is home!

The wind blows

Birds sing

And the flowers bloom

No walls of bondage

Filled with midnite cries of gloom

Mentally I'm free…

To laugh with my sistas

Hug my mother

Visit my brother

And give myself to my lover

No khakis, sweats or Deptcor merchandise in my sight

I have not 1

But 6 pillows

For my comfort at night

Satin sheets for a Queen on my king size bed

Adorned by the loveliest scents and quilted spread

Not the wool itchy shit

That they give us instead

I possess my own keys

To come and go as I please

For here I am the Queen

With no burdens or worries

Becuz my Lord truly supplies all of my needs

Mentally I'm free...

To laugh, dance, praise and sing

As the Lord blesses my womb

With an innocent side of me

My thoughts, my thoughts

Are so very far from this place

For to be mentally in bondage

Is certainly a disgrace

But my Lord

In all of His love, mercy and grace

Has brought me thus far along this journey

And that is why I still have faith

Mentally I'm free

Mentally I'm free

Mentally I'm free

With God on my side

Why wouldn't I be?

Life

The best things in life are free

Freedom, love, sex and peace

Freedom is beautiful

For God created the world for us all to explore

That is why it is my belief

That it's inhumane to be caged behind a locked door

Love is love

Yet only when it's real

It can give life to a lonely soul

Or be the dagger to make hearts stand still

Sex is awesome!

For through it's conception

We all came to be

Not to mention the creativity within it

That takes me to ecstasy

Peace is self explanatory

For it comes from God alone

And it is that peace

That keep us sane

Until we're called to heaven our home

Where I'm From

I'm from African mate dances and circumcision

Flames from the fires

That burn your vision

I'm from cotton picking

And sugar canes

Blood, sweat, tears

And dry birth pains

Where I'm from?

Do you really want to know?

I'm from food stamps

And ass whippings

Broken glass

And news paper clippings

Bamboo earrings

With Jherri curls dripping

Free lunches in the summer

And fire hydrants soak and wet

Step shows and slap boxing

In the name of respect

I'm from taking the A train Uptown

For $15 doobies

Giving fake numbers

To the cornballs and groupies

I'm from fist fights with razor blades

Gun hots and pepper spray
I'm from wearing a bulletproof vest
When you dress
Poverty, Murda, Violence
And never a moment to rest!

Final Tears

Do not trust the world

For the world cannot be trusted

They deceive, betray, lie and cheat

Only to leave you disgusted

Some say that "it's better to have loved and lost

Than never to have loved at all"

Well, I say:

"It's better to have real love hold you up

When so many plot on your fall"

But what is one to do

When the one you gave your heart too

After 6 long years

No longer belongs to you

How did we get here

When did you really decide

To stomp on my fragile heart

And make your mistress your bride

All I can say to that is WHOA

Who you are?

I really don't know

These are my final tears

Becuz tonight

I'm really letting go

It's funny becuz after you faded

I still entertained thoughts of us
But your decision to wife that cum dumpster
Has left me in disgust
How could you do this to me?
I thought your love was so profound
All I did was love and support you
When no one else was around
She could NEVER be me
Just like the next could never be you
You can lie to yourself if you want
But the bitch in ya bed…
She is not ya Pooh!

Fear Of Imprisonment

I've always been one who feared loneliness, yet crave

solitude

Never cared for the crowds or to be in the spotlight

For my presence is felt

Wherever I am

Whether loved or hated

I continue to stand

However, my fear of imprisonment

Ironically led me to exist within a prison in my mind

Living the life of an outlaw...

Runnin, runnin & runnin

No justice

No peace

No future

No release

Just fast cars, sex, money, pills and weed

Headed nowhere fast

Misguided, mistreated and misunderstood

While living each day as my last

Melting clocks

Becuz I'm runnin out of time

This fear of imprisonment

Had me out of my mind

Runnin, druggin, thuggin and buggin

Led me down a path of self-destruction

Numbing the pain

With every stroke

From the stranger in my bed

While the fear of imprisonment

Fucks with my head

Paranoia at its best

With every passing siren

No sleep and no rest

Wiretaps

Informants

Helicopters up top

Handcuffs

Walkie talkies

And detectives circling the block

Still runnin

Still thuggin

Still druggin

"Jazz is buggin" they say

That is until that dreadful day

They set me up to be taken away

Now who buggin?

No more runnin

Becuz my fear of imprisonment has come to pass

No designer labels, fast cars, dick and weed

Alone in a cell

With this little blue book
And no one to talk with me
Newspaper clippings
Snake ass lawyers
Betrayal and
Lies, lies, lies
Bullpens, bullshit, strip searches
And a helpless mother cries
It is here
That my deepest fear
Became more clear
For what I thought was the end
Turned out to be my beginning
And now again the end is near
Eight years later
Much stronger, wiser and greater
Indeed I've conquered my biggest fear
For when I was weak I became strong
And it's only by the grace and mercy of God
That I'm still here!

Fuckin Da System

As I sit in this cell

Lookin over my life

So much hurt, disappointment

Heartache and strife

I wonder if God knew

That things will turn out this way

That I'd be stuck in the system

Fighting to see the light of day

I tried to do things their way

But when I do and did

I still find myself

With the short end of the stick

My son is dead

And I miscarried the twins

My soul got lost

Living a life filled with sin

My mental was twisted

With only money on my mind

It's survival of the fittest

So I stay on the grind

To get rich or die trying

While inside my soul is dying

Mommas crying

And my co-dees steady lying

They put the blame on me
As if I'm dat chic
Who put the gun to his head
And made the trigger go "click"
On the real I'm only guilty of loving the dick
Of a hustler turned hitman
Ain't that some shit
Now he's six feet under
And I'm doing his time
Over a decade later
Still fighting for mines
Will I ever get to see
The productive side of me
Free from my sins
The shame and pain
And what about the fame
In a world where everybody knows your face
They can GOOGLE a diva
And check the D.O.C. web space
The picture is just what you want it to be
Some see a menace
While others, the innocent side of me
The face that's screaming
"Save me from this beast"
Laugh now
Cry later

I told yall mutts it wasnt me

On the flip side, I'm in here

Just trying to make it

To rise above oppression

But my life

Yall trying to take it

So what the fuck do you want me to do

Bend over and let you fuck me

Becuz you wearing blue

Nah, I'm gonna fuck you too

And I'm not staying in this place

Yall fucking me against my will

And if you aint know they call that rape

You're holding me down

And forcing yourself on me

I'm screaming for Help

But even that bitch ignoring me

So what's a diva to do

But seduce ya own kind

Lure them into my web

And have 'em think they got my mind

Turn 'em into a mule

And make'em love me long time

Now yall mad

Lookin at me all screw faced in shit

You can pull ya skirt down now

Cuz I'm done wit ya trick

See, I wasn't turned out

I was raised this way

Mama told me

"When they hit you hit'em back

Never turn or walk away"

So excuse me if I don't apologize for my actions

Now we both got a nutt

So it's a mutual satisfaction!

BaBa Don't Leave

(4 Dad)

BaBa don't leave

I need you right now

BaBa stay strong

Hold ya head

Dust off ya crown

You can make it through this storm

It may seem cloudy now

But a rainbow will soon form

BaBa dont leave

I need you there when I come home

BaBa I love you

And I need you in my life

BaBa I'm sorry

For the years lost, pain and strife

BaBa don't leave

I wanna make you proud

BaBa don't leave

I cannot deal with this now

Not here

Not like this

Not in this beast

Not in this pit

Daddy, I love you

Please don't go

"Stay strong" you say

And that It's gonna be okay

But for once Dad you're wrong

I'm not

Becuz you're all I got

So please don't leave ya baby girl

In this cold, cold world ALONE!!!

Convo with God

I'm in love

In love with who?

In love with you

In love with me

Yes you!

But why me?

Becuz you're You...

I love you too!

Misunderstood

Save me O'Lord

Please come take my hand

I am surrounded by mortals

Who just don't understand

They rather tear you down

And scheme on what they can get

Than to stop and see what makes you exist...

Diva, hold ya head

For you weren't built to break

If they aint for you they against you

So fuck'em

They so fake

There is life outside of this place

And this right here

Is only a temporary state

Don't you ever forget

You are a warrior Queen

And yes,

The fight is worth it

Freedom is near

And baby, you deserve it!

OUT

I'm bothered right now

I'm going through some shit

I'm searching my heart

And question if it's really worth it

I done prayed and cried

Cried and prayed

I promised to love you forever

But it's like diggin my own grave

Inside I'm slowly dying

As I hold the fight steady trying

I'm sick of crying!

And getting ya ass to kiss in return

Maybe I should be like Usher

And let it burn, baby burn

Perhaps we have already

Seen our better days

I'm so true to you

Yet with my heart you continue to play

I've been on my Jodeci ish

And decided to "Stay"

"Forever Your Lady"

But even with that you act so shady

What's happened to us baby?

There's a stranger in my house

I'm sick of writing these love poems
And you careless what their about
I'm so tired of ya dirty ass
And so now I'm really out!!!

Changes

Damn, Shawty got me stressing

Sitting in lock-up I miss ya

Crying

Missing ya presence

Ya texts and ya pictures

You told me not to let this system get me under suspicion

I thought if you left me

It'll be for somebody that's thicker

The rain is coming down

And I swear it's my sorrow

As I wipe the tears away

I take a look and see tomorrow

I'm gonna make it

Even if I gotta beg and borrow

Reading ya love letters late night

Locked down and quiet

If bitches don't receive our mail

Better believe we riot

Eating bread and butter

While staring at these walls of silence

Inside this cage

Where they captured all of my rage and violence

Indeed I learned some true lessons

Caught up in this system

All I got is God, myself

And my pain is my wisdom

Right now it is what it is

So I'm gonna make it do what it do

Almost 10 years later

And I'm still in love with you

Now that's crazzzy

Through all the pain and strife

Whoever would have thought ya Pooh

Wouldn't be ya first official wife

Now, don't get mad

I'm only spitting what I feel

What ya life like my dude

Cuz my shit stay raw and real

But you know the deal

Cuz you aint a stranger to this beast

As a matter of fact

You the same joker who schooled me

And hip me to the fakes

How to shake the jakes

But in the end

It was you who turned into the snake

It hurt so bad

You could hear my heart break

But it's all G

Cuz you still my boo

And I know without a doubt

I will always love you

Even though

You're sleeping with the enemy

The bitch in ya bed

Is really ya frenemy

Can't you see

That she want to be me

Out there living my life

And the trifling ass whore

Ain't even doing that right

Man, she don't wanna see me

On any level

I'll crucify her ass

Have her thinking I'm the devil

Straight up leave her mind disheveled

Like a middle eastern rebel

Hell no

I aint off dat

Cuz I'll see her one day

Dressed in all black

On some face to face shit

To really see where her heart at

If you knew like I know

You'll fall back

And avoid her like the plague

Cuz they will

And have too

Free Da'Diva one day
Nah, I ain't just talking smack
Becuz of where I'm at
Or the lump in my throat
I promise you baby
That this right here
Is the realest shit I ever wrote!

Visions

I see visions for a reason

For everything has a season

A time to plant

And a time for the harvest

You reap what you sow

It's gonna happen regardless

As for me

I just lay in this prison bed

As visions of greatness

Flow through my head

Yes, I can finally see

Myself living out my destiny

Despite where I am

It hasn't gotten the best of me

My visions are great

Ad they only get greater

They may seem far fetched to some

But that's what we call a hater

Hi hater

Bye hater

For all things are possible

With my Maker

Indeed the Lord has brought me this far

Not to leave nor forsake me

But strengthen my heart

As I stay focused on the cross

I can finally see the light

And step out of the dark

Visions are hope

In times of adversity

One must have faith

And that takes audacity

Not measured by one's own mental capacity

But to trust in God's infinite strategy

With knowing that things

Are much closer than they seem

My God says:

"Write the vision and make it plain"

For its more than just a dream!

Loving Me

With a gold mine between my thighs

I embrace what God gave me

From my fat toes to brown eyes

Much to my own surprise

I have evolved three times over

And continue to rise

Above the stereo -types in the hood

Street savvy indeed

But trust it's all good

As I continue to stride

With my head held high

And much pride

Definitely more than a dime

My worth is priceless

Lifestyle righteous

Please believe

There's not many like this

I'm the original Jazz

With a phat ass

But don't get it twisted

Cuz ya girl got class

Versatile with it

Free styles

I can spit it

With the bigwigs I politic

No matter where I'm at

Trust I'm always Dat chic

Locked down for a while

But I'm still moving forward

I gotta big ego

But hey, I can afford it

My beauty is captivating

Yall wish you can ignore it

Nah, I'm not cocky

Just confident for a reason

I'm loving myself hard

And if you aint know it's my season

To live up to my potential

And truly live my life

The world is a stage

And you only get one mic

So I'm gonna make it do what it do

Like I always do and did

Rise above oppression

And say good-bye to this bid

Dat Chic

They ain't been where I been

Or seen what I seen

So how can I expect for them to recognize a Queen

On the murda scene

Smoking that sticky green

With dem white boys in my system

Made it all a dream…

I woke up

To pink faces and handcuffs

Coroner photos

With the D.A. trying to gas me up

"Drop a dime on dem niggas

Or we'll lock ya ass up!"

Now I'm on the back of the bus

On my way to prison

Am I still dreaming

Or is this reality I'm living

I ask myself

How did it get to this

Caught up in the beast

For the cold and heartless

I ain't the one to start shit

But I'm the one to finish

It's crazy when the one I rode for

Is the D.A. star witness
Now on me you flip the script?
When I was always Dat Chic
With the full clip
And tight grip
Ready to pull dat shit
Yo shit is crazy
Ain't no love
When you trying to fade me
The game ain't make me baby
I made the game
But it's insane
When the ones you ride for
Are the ones to bring you pain
Now tear drop stains
Are engraved on my heart
Bitch, how you gonna cross the one
Who put you on from the start
Now you's the mark
Expendable you are
And me
I'm still dat shining star
And will continue to shine
Locked down for a while
But only get better with time
Still penning them rhymes

And extended the resume

Cuz the system can't get credit

For who I am today

I was born this way

It's my destiny

And honey I refuse

To let this shit get the best of me

Trust, I will always stand tall

No matter where I'm at

I'm Dat Chic on the top bunk

With the cell stashed in the matt

Straight sipping Grey Goose in water bottles

My style you try to follow

But can't keep up

I real live guerillas in the cut

Who don't give a fuck

One stroke of my pen

They'll light ya whole family up

So don't sleep

On the Jesus piece

Or becuz I'm calm and meek

Trust there's another side

That you have yet to see

Will put you to sleep with the quickness

Handling my bizness

With a vengeance

Have you begging and pleading
Asking for forgiveness
What is this?
I thought you was gangsta-born tough
Ya style is wack
War stories made up
Straight taking notes
From all them hood books you read
Bitch I was getting money
While you was in the bed
Dreaming of Santa Claus
While I'm in the fast cars
Under the stars
With a G-pack stashed in my bra
Big Willy's trying to get in my drawls
And wife me up
With diamonds and baguettes
No doubt, I'm Dat Chic
They never could forget
The leather interior
Keep my pussy wet
Bust my guns for the hood
In the name of respect
Nah, I ain't boasting
Just keeping it real
So next time you question my existence

You'll know the deal

And all of this

Ain't even the half

To sum it up

I'm "DAT CHIC"

AKA

"Da'Diva Jazz"

Wake Up

I'm thinking of George Jackson now
He is you and he is me
And every colored face
In the walls of the beast
And those who walk the streets
Vulnerable to the accepted norms of this perverse society
Where aborting black babies is cool
Killin ya brother is even better
Disrespecting the women
And no desires to stick together
Miseducating our youth
With bullshit curriculums
While the blood of our ancestors cries out for the truth
From the wet loam
They were brutally forced to tend too
With stripes on their backs
Born males under attack
Brainwashed to feel inferior
So they won't react to the strap
It all makes me think back
To the seed of my own womb
And if in fact
They were in harm's way
By man's prenatal care

It boggles me
That in doing so they're no longer here
But were victims to the greatest conspiracy
To eradicate the hierarchies fear
Of the black man
How strong and beautiful he stands
With vehemence in his eyes
And prowess engraved in his hands
The epitome of love
Manifested in flesh and bone
But love goes out the window
When they are taken out of the home
And forced to exist
Within the confines of the pit
For the cold and heartless
They weren't born this way
Society made 'em like this
Raping their women
Stripping their identity
Selling their children
And cheating them from making a decent living
I swear, this capitalist society makes me vexed
Instead of more schools
Their funding wars, prisons and projects
While teaching our children
To accept disrespect…

Barbed wire, broken glass

Hungry cries and young boys selling dope

Lying politicians with no health care

And minimum wage is a joke

Broken families give up hope

Becoming a product of their environment

For my people

There is no such thing as early retirement

Mama working 3 jobs

And selling dinner plates just to make ends meet

Newspaper clippings and R.I.P. shirts

Of the man-child shot dead in the street

Rest In Peace

But we're living in pieces

It's time to wake up

Where are our righteous teachers

We're losing our people

Am I the only one who see this?

Disdain

The words spit from your lips

Like a dagger piercing my soul

Ripping through to the core of my being

Leaving me forsaken

Vulnerable, bleeding and seething

With my wounded heart barely breathing

How can you claim to love me

And such things come about

The coldness of your words

Fills me with doubts

If destiny will be manifested

Or if I should go another route

You claim to be different

But I see that's a lie

Becuz just like the rest

You have made me cry

Which brings me to the conclusion

That your species is all the same

On a mission to conquer one's heart

And bring nothing but hurt and pain

So with that said, just know

That at this moment

It is you that I truly disdain!

Presence

I still recall the taste of your tears
Your voice echoes
Just like a ringing in my ears
My favorite dreams
Of you still wash ashore
Dominating my thoughts
Until I can't take no more
I feel you with me everyday
So close but so far
When I close my eyes and listen
I can hear you with every beat of my heart
Sometimes it sings a song
All of its own
Of a love so profound
Craving for home
And then there's the times
My heart just cries
Wondering if you are unfaithful to me
And hurting me more with your lies
Why baby why
Must I feel these things
Your presence is with me always
But it's you with another that really stings…

Just

Just love me

Need me

Want me

Please me

Touch me

Tease me

Tell me

Kiss me

Exhale me

Let me

Come get me

Sweat me

Don't regret me

Simply

Just

Us!

Don't Judge Me

Life through my eyes
Would scare the average to death
I done seen and been through so much
And rocked with the best
Shed tears from my soul
Until there's nothing left
Done cried and prayed
Prayed and cried
Even tried to numb the pain I feel inside
While watching the years of my youth pass by
Please don't judge me
Until you've seen life through my eyes
Tell me,
Have you ever seen a grown man cry
Or know what it's like to hold a dead baby
And witness your own earth
Slowly go crazy
With knowing that you are the cause of the pain and
frustration
The feelings of helplessness and despair
Is a conflicting situation
As you compromise your destiny
Pissed the hell off
That these pigs got the best of me

So please don't whisper or stare

Neither pretend that you care

Until you've life through these bloodshot eyes

And know how I really got here!

WTF?

Hate seeking revenge

Is love really a friend

Or more or less a foe

In a place where mere mortals don't know

Who

What

When or where

Or perhaps they do

And just don't care

Man, I'm telling you

I gotta get outta here!

Da Struggle Continues

(For those chained with me and the pig who set me up)

(North Corridor Lock-Up)

My conscience calls as I sit in this cell looking over my life. I find myself in a place of familiarity. I've been here before; three walls and a door. Once again caged with my rage, frustrations, pain and the optimistic side of me.

"Keep ya head up, stay strong, positive and have faith".

These are the things that I tell myself daily. Yet, I am continuously consumed by the pessimistic forces that exist within the confines of my surroundings. This brings me into a war in my mind battling against my soul and bringing me deeper into captivity.

What is justice?

Where is lady liberty?

That bitch needs glasses

Because Stevie Wonder can see this shit just aint right

Yet still I continue to fight to rise above oppression and find a better way

With Panther blood pumping through my veins

I am weak as though I've been fighting for many moons

Even as I spill my ink I am captive

A P.O.W.

A battle ignited before my existence but even so

The struggle continues as I hold up the torch passed down
to me from generations past
No doubt, I know when to cut up
As well as when to shut the fuck up
But why should I?
I'm sorry but Mama ain't raise no coward
"Patience taken too far is cowardice"
I'm so radical
On this modern day plantation
They don't know how to take me
Sorry, but your whip ain't thick enough
The blows don't even fade me any more
I'm immune to this shit now and refuse to conform
To these plantation norms and perversity
I'm not ya mammie, nigger or "crack whore" as you so
eloquently put it
Please tell me why you're so mad?
Is it my beauty or the booty you'll never get
Or is it becuz I am just Dat Chic
You envy me
My prowess, passion and even the pain that birthed the
crown of wisdom adorned with much pride
I've always been the shit
And you?
You must be worthless
Since oppressing another is what hardens your dick

U R SICK

Check yourself Mr. Smurf in a skirt

Or you will continue to be checked

By one of the best

Yes

I

Me

One of the last a dying breed

J-A Double Z

FAGGOT!!!!!

My Mama

(For Sandra Faye AKA Mama Faraha)
Krazy
Unique
Beautiful
Mystique
Full of life
Love and Pain
You were with us for while
Our memories will always
Make me smile
Your voice and laughter
Stays in my head
You live on in our hearts
So you'll never be dead
I love you Mommy!!!!

Dear Mama

Dear Mama, got me missin you

Ya sweet and tender touch

Ya smile

Ya laughter

And how I love you so much

Never thought I'd see the day

When our times are no more

Got a diva coming home

With no parents to look for

I can't even deny

That at times I sit back and cry

Trying to keep my composure

But still asking God why

It's like all that I love

Get taken away

My babies

My freedom

Malii

And now Faye

Damn

It gotta be a better way

I'm down here on this earth

With so much love in my heart

Yet I always get hurt

With my shit ripped apart

Whether it's betrayal, deception or death

Shit is a mess

But I'm a hold my head

Til my last breath

And never surrender

Or settle 4 less!

Pain

My Mama and my BaBa gone

Now I'm on my own

In this cold, cruel world

All alone

So fly and so grown

In a zone

Time made me strong

I've been doing this shit for years

Shed so many tears

And watched my greatest fears

Slowly but surely appear

Back to back

Shit serious like a heart attack

I want my life back

To when it didn't hurt so much

And it was all good

Even when we didn't have a lot

Understanding was understood

That with the sunshine it has to rain

I used to feel so much love

And now my life is filled with pain

Tear drop stains

All over my chest

I'm trying my best

Not to stress

But trust in God

And see my prayers manifest

Lord knows

I can stand to be blessed

And finally put this pain to rest!

Intercession

(For Jamie Farthing)

I cried for you
And you didn't even know it
I can feel your pain
Although you don't show it
I pray for you
Becuz I see the potential you possess
Your uniqueness
Creativity, humor, your diligence and prowess
I ask the Lord to restore
All of the years that you've fought
Never mind what the judge said
For it is with the blood of Christ
You've been bought
You are a new creation
Therefore, old things have passed away
I don't know what led you here
But I do know that it's not in His will to stay
The circumstances doesn't even matter
Just continue to seek His face
My sister you have people praying for you
So stay strong and keep the faith….
I'm praying for you!

Untitled

(For those who still believe in love)

Love & Lovers
In secret making magic
Under the stars of rhythm
Swift and sweet
Hard and rough
Like a flame to a fire
That can't get enough
The stinging tears of passion
Aggressively surfaces
With each thrust
As our bodies entwine
You groan in triumph
Your voice
Slick and sleek
Your flesh
Dark and deep
Perfectly seasoned
Just for me
Now and forever
Forever and always
In the fields of passion
Love and lovers

In and out of time
Time and time again
I am yours
And you are mines!

Liberation

A February afternoon with trees naked and bare
Much like a repentant heart
Before the Lord in times of despair
Does anyone care about the clothes she wears
How she styles her hair
Or if the judge was fair
Her lover miles away
Another place
Another state
Shit, even another case
It's been twelve years
Since she sat on his face
He desires to penetrate
To the very core of her being
She reciprocates
And acknowledge a love so freeing
Liberation in the midst of incarceration
Along with the manifestation
Of true love in its purest form
As she sits and meditates
On all of the years she's been gone
Expressing herself
In the form of a poem

On the top bunk all alone

In a zone

Nine years in prison

And damn, she's grown

Naked and exposed

Like Lil Kim's left breast

Home girl done been through it

Some shit she will never forget

Chin up, chest out

With much pride

Nothing to hide

As she continues to stride

With God on her side

She's baaaad!

And she's coming out

With no worries or doubts

But ambition and much clout

You'll see what she's about

With all of her wisdom learned through pain

But it's her faith

That has kept her sane

And now she's liberated

To dance in the rain

Go on Diva

And do the damn thang!

Empty Love

I felt empty love as I ran the streets

Seeking, searching and yearning

For someone or something to validate me

To numb the pain and take me away

To another place

To a better day

I felt empty love

With the hole in my heart

And the emptiness of my womb

With eyes bloodshot red

Witnessing a part of me in a tomb

This emotion non-existent

As I poison my body with drugs

Pills, weed, liquor and wet

All the while looking for love

But there are no hugs

For a thug misses

Only a couple thrusts

Topped with sloppy kisses

As I give myself to another

Whose name I'd soon forget

I blink and it's over

As I find myself before a white man in a black dress

I stand there broken but not shattered

Silently praying for a way out of this mess

It is when I confess

With belief in my heart that my Savior came through

And that my dear

Is right then and there

That my love was renewed…

Thank you Jesus!

The Erotica

The erotica for me

Is to be

Brought to climax without sex

As a potential lover makes love to my mind

As well as to feel him

Next to me, inside, on top and behind

Pulling my hair

Whispering in my ear

And sending tingles down my spine

Our bodies entwined

As the two become one flesh

Producing a product of our love

To nurse upon my breasts

But hold up

I'm not done yet…

The erotica for me

Would also be

To publish my books

And write a good poem

To eat mint chocolate chip ice-cream

Dance in the rain

And to walk around naked in my own home

To drive down the freeway

Ninety miles per hour

Top down and music up

Screaming out "Black Power"

Longevity, diversity, intricacy mixed with intimacy

As I cast aside the restrictions

Placed on me by society

Indeed all of the above

Are things that I love

And are definitely worth wild

But what I really want and desire

Is to live up to my potential

And make my Shero proud!

Genesis of Captivity

In the beginning there was nothing
Solitude, hurt, pain and despair
Betrayal, disappointments
And not too many who really care
Phoniness and lies
No answer to midnight cries
Oh I thought I would die
From the emptiness inside
Ain't no pride with loneliness as your only friend
But when shit hits the fan
And the walls are closing in
Where do I really begin
The voices in my head
Calling my name
The voices of the dead
I think I'm going insane...
SAG teams
Court rooms
Bullpens
And Goon squads
The devil has blue eyes
Supposed to be on my side
But he's robbing my gramma blind!

Mister Man

You walk with a limp
And talk all of that hot shit
Licking ya lips
And grabbing ya dick
Yet, when it's time to man up
Ya actions straight contradict
Everything you spit
About loving me right
And going the distance
Ya style aint consistent
And you wonder
Why I'm so resistant
To go all in
And give you my heart
How can I trust you
When you don't even play ya part
See, I'm a real woman
And that lame game don't go far
I'm walking in the light
And you lost in the dark
I try to upgrade you
And take you places you places you never been
You want me as wife
But can't even take me as friend

I'm trying to live righteous

And you're comfortable in sin

Man, when it comes to you

I don't know where to begin

Lost Love

When the one you love
No longer loves you back
Let'em go
And see how they react
If it's meant to be
Then they will come back
But it's up to you
How to deal with that
Be smart
Be strong
To thy own self be true
If you aint break by now
Then you'll make it thru
And at the end of the day
If the love is really gone
You didn't really lose
Becuz something better will come along
One day
Some day
When you least expect it
It may not be who you want right now
But at least you're respected

Stuck

Dem streets don't love nobody

But everybody love the streets

It's a war out there

But they searching for peace

Niggas cased up

Staying laced up

Will whip out a ratchet

Before a pay stub

Niggas stay stuck

Coming home from doing a grip

To homies out there

Doing the same old shit

Talking about it's hard to go legit

But be the same ones in the county

Ready to flip

Now you tell me

Who's really the bitch?

F.E.B.

Feels like my brain is on fire

Mental ejaculation

Takes me higher

Got me ready to retire

But I gotta stay strong

And prove the devil a liar

Shit is real

And oh so serious

I spill my ink

And tears shed

For those that's curious

They tried to fade me

And now they're furious

Mental rape

Be the case

Leaving the haters straight delirious

Fuck Every Body!

Things I Miss

Mamas smile
G-ma's cooking
Children laughter
Stealing the car keys
And the wrath that comes right after
Sitting on the porch smoking on goods
With the Remy flowing through me
Got a diva twerking on that wood
Damn, I wish I could
I miss chillin in the G-ryde
With my closest road dawg by my side
Looking all fly
As we laugh and joke around
Steady getting high
On cloud nine
Leaving these earthlings behind
I really miss those times…
I'm in my own zone
Wishing for home
I'm so sick of these people
With their phony smiles and agendas
This mundane love shit
When I really am a winner
I deserve so much more

Than this place has to offer

I want out so bad

If you feel me come and holla

At ya gal trapped in this beast

I done been through so much

Someone please come and save me

I miss waking up in my own bed

As thoughts of the night before

Flow through my head

Damn, how I could be dead

Yes, I'm certainly aware

But right now death calling me

Gotta be better than in here!

Just One of Dem Days

I can't do you
No, not today
Your insecurities
And made up illusions
Are just in the way
Blocking my blessings
Clarity and judgement
I need peace of mind
Not all of the fighting and fussing
Over nothing!
The pessimism and arrogance
Is just not my thing
I'm an optimistic, free spirit
Who desires beautiful things
I see so much in you
Yet, you chose to give me the worse
It's as if you're a blessing
Transforming into a curse
What planet are you from?
So smart but so dumb
I'm not beat to figure you out
Becuz today
I AM NOT THE ONE!!!

A Diva's Prayer

You, Oh Lord hold the heart of the King right in Your hand

Like the rivers of water

It turns wherever You command

So on this day

Lord, I sincerely pray

For You to soften the judges heart

And make a way

To restore my precious life

From the enemy's plan

For You alone are God

In comparison, none can withstand

Your mercy, grace, truth and glory

I thank You for intervening

And turning around my story

That was once one of self-destruction

Your chastisement was needed

So I don't rebuke correction

But I thank You for Your infinite wisdom

Oh, how I look forward

To inheriting Your kingdom

For this is the promise to those who call on You

I thank You for that

And ask that You answer this earthly prayer too

Remember those chained with me

In the belly of the beast

Judge each one according to their hearts

And grant us thy release

In Jesus name. Amen

Deja Vu

The burning bush

Broken idols

Withered fig tree

The brook

I've been here before

Fire by night

Clouds by day

Fresh manna from above

Strengthening me along the way

Whispers in the wind

The sparrows fly & sing

I'm going around the mountain again

What does this all mean?

I've been here before

In the wilderness of bondage

Diligently seeking

The Land of Promise

I know that He is faithful

And will never steer me wrong

Yet, I find myself here once again

Singing the same old song

Praying for forgiveness

While trying to find my way

"Lord please help me"

Is what I daily pray

I'm going around the mountain one more time

Please dear Lord, direct my paths

And keep my soul as well as my mind

I need you Jesus!

Heaven Gates

I close my eyes and shut my ears

And I swear I feel you near

Being my motivation

Just to make it out of here

"Be good, stay strong and get home"

Is what you told me

But we never talked about

Just who's gonna hold me

Through these stressful times

When I think about you

Sometimes it's unreal

It's almost 2 years without you

You was always so real

That even in death I can't doubt you

I gotta express myself

So yo, I'm about too…

I love you

I miss you

I wanna hug you

And kiss you

Tell you about my day

As you laugh at my issues

I wanna hear ya voice

I wanna see ya smile

I wanna get the time back

Cuz I been gone a long while

No doubt, I am my mama's child

And that's something that the state can't take

But God took you from me

I'm just sorry He didn't wait

Don't get me wrong

Cuz me and G straight

I can't be mad at the Man

In whom hands hold my fate

I'm just saying that I miss you

And my Mama I will always appreciate

Shout out to all the mothers

Waiting at Heaven Gates!

Happy Mothers Day Mommy!

Neglected

I walk with my head up

And smile

When I really want to cry

No one really knows all of the pain

That I hold inside

But when I let down my guard

To open my heart

It hurts when that person

Just doesn't get that part

Mistreated and misunderstood

Is what I am

I give myself to you

But tell me

Do you really give a damn?

Remember The Time

I can remember the time

When my time was your time

And your time was my time

The time we made time

And spent time

Building our foundation

Every second, minute and hour of time

Yes that was the time

When I honestly believed the time

Even though what we shared

Could stand the test of times

But then there came the time

Which broke the time

And we stopped making time

Time together

Was is wasted time?

And now are we stuck in time?

Time will tell it all

But please just tell me

Do you remember the time?

Miss Me

You're only still here becuz when you strayed

I stayed and never left you

You showed ya ass

But I still saw the best in you

Made up excuses

Justifying ya shit

I remained by ya side

Becuz I thought you was worth it

And now here we are

Once again

At the crossroads of life

Same game just a different chic

And here I stand the good wife

Maybe if I was a hoe

I would have the strength

To let you go

And then maybe you'd act right

And recognize the real Queen

You had in ya life

Man, I don't know

I'm just tired of writing these sad ass poems

But on thing I know for sure

You gonna miss me when I'm gone!

Mirror Mirror

When I see you
I see me
And all that I was
Created to be
My purpose
My gift
My wish come true
So many days and nights
That I prayed for you
My subconscious takes over
When you do me wrong
Make a diva start trippin
Like it's me all along
But the devil is a liar
Becuz for our love
I been walked through the fire
And stayed true
Despite all of the bullshit
That you put me through
I stood by you
And yes, I still do
While others judge
Hold a grudge
And mad cuz I didn't fuck

On the one I love

But instead of you seeing my worth

You try to play me to the left

And put my name in the dirt

Sometimes I think

That you like seeing me hurt

I swear ya skitzoness

Gonna drive me berserk

Fuckin jerk!

Fuck All Y'all

Fuck these bitches

All of these bitches

They can keep they mind on me

But they can't do shit to me

That's why they all just stare at me

Peeking like I can't see…

I bet the D.A.

Thought they had me in the grave

Didn't think that I would make it

To see the light of day

But I did

I'm here

I made it through the storm

Pushing through the pain

And I'm still standing strong

Even though so many

Tried to do me wrong

I'm still a Queen on my throne

And at the top is where I belong

I'm making it

I'm almost there

The end is near

Shit ain't dim no more

The pictures real clear

So they can picture me rollin

Right up and outta these gates

Fuck all of yall

I'm getting money

So stay the hell out my face!

What's Next?

Thing thing called life is deep

It's like you reach a point

Where you've been through too much to go back

And at times, too much to go forward

Yet you press on

Indeed, with all of one's wisdom learned through pain

Ultimately it shapes who you have evolved to become

Even so, please tell me

What's next?

I mean, what's next in a world

That judges you by the color of your skin, gender, social

class and flaws

A world that cares less about your hopes and dreams

But focuses on the law

Making and breaking their own rules

In a game of win, lose or draw

What's next

For someone who was born a Queen

Yet forced to live a life of hardship and despair

With your innocence stolen

As you deal with things you should not bare

Sex, drugs, violence

And your heart broken and shattered

Watching your shero chase an invisible dragon

As if that's all that matters

Whats next

When your very existence is defined

By one love, one night, one ride

One shot, one breath and dude died

Like what are you supposed to do

When someone who doesn't even know who you are

Has authority over your life and liberty

No doubt,

You throw on a good suit and shoes

As you stand before this white man in a black dress

He doesn't even acknowledge your existence

For you're nothing more than a docket number on his desk

Yes! One less nigger-bitch in society

As the hired gun besides you shoot blanks

It's all a charade

Becuz they already know your fate

"It's a fuckin conspiracy"

You scream

Ready to hit the fence

Knowing this cracker about to smoke you with time

That just doesn't make sense

Shiiit

I'm convinced

The devil has blue eyes

And sits behind the bench

Your favorite lady sits there
Doing all that she can to get you out of this mess
While inside her heart is breaking
And ain't no mistaking
The tear drop stains on her dress
Although she tries to keep the faith
In the courtroom
The only colored face
Even she knows your fate
Yet she continues to pray
For her grandchild to see the light of day
What's next when after so many years
You're still in the same situation
Flooded with tears
The kids are grown now
And Gramma grey hairs turned white
Pops can barely walk
But he's holding up the fight
Mom's a hypochondriac
Welcoming defeat
And the prison grape vine buzzin
With all eyes on me
"It's something about her"
They whisper and stare
"Yeah, I know bitches,
I don't really belong here"

But what's really next for a diva
Who is against all odds?
Keep shining
Stay focused
And give it to God!
This too shall pass

Exclusive

If you love me
Say it
If you want me
Take it
If you crave me
Cake it...
Ain't no pride
To what I'm feeling inside
Cuz baby, I'm a woman about mines
Plus I can see it in ya eyes
Staring at my thick ass thighs
Watching ya manhood rise
As I lick my lips
Seductively asking
"Do you like it like this"
Ass cheek naked
In 5 inch heels
I;m a shorty for real
But don't sleep
Cuz I can handle the steel
Plus hook up a meal
Yea, baby you know the deal
Nah, I aint stunting and fronting
Cuz it's you I'm wanting

Just the thought of you
Got my clit throbbing and jumping
Squirming in my seat
You would think I was buggin
Or maybe I am
Fantasizing about a man
So close but so far
I just dont understand
No doubt, fate got jokes
Like Martin Lawrence on coke
But I'm determined about mines
So I'm going for broke
Moaning and groaning
Throwing it back with each stroke
No, it ain't just about sex
Although I can't help
That you keep me wet
But it's everything about you
I love and respect
Well almost everything
Becuz there's more to explore
But what I'm saying is that
You got me
And it's you that I adore
You haven't even touched me
And I'm craving for more

Face down

Ass up

As you enter my back door

Pulling my hair

And biting me on the shoulder

Smacking my ass

Screaming out "girl I told ya"

Damn, Daddy you a soulja

Now lay back and let me ride you

Like a real woman supposed too

You flip me over

And I climb on top

Cowgirl style ass backwards

Mmm baby that's my spot

Up and down

In and out

I'll make it clap for you baby

And let you see what I'm about

You're moaning my name

And I know you about to cum

But hold up baby

Cuz ya Queen aint done

Without hesitation I jump off the dick

I wanna taste you so bad

I take you in my lips

And now as I feel ya shaft down my throat

Got me hummin a tune

That Beyonce wrote

Dangerously in Love

You got me ready to choke

But as I told you before

I'm going for broke

Go hard or go home

You got me in a zone

I feel you tense up

And now I know it's on

You grab my head

And push deeper in ya lap

Working my throat muscles

I feel you climax

I love you long time

And that's a fact

Biting ya bottom lip

With ya eyes closed and toes curled

With ya seed in my system

You're forever my baby

And I'm forever ya girl…

Welcome to my world!!!

The Majority

Pickin my afro
And pumpin my fist
We've been oppressed for too long
It's time we surfaced
Above the psycho chains of slavery and statistics
Black, yellow, brown and red
We must learn to co-exist
And let our actions be consistent
As we press forward
We all must be persistent
For a house divided cannot stand
"Power" belongs to all humanity
Not just the white man
They call us a minority
Becuz we don't agree
With capitalizing from another's poverty
But when you take off the blinders
We are in fact the majority
If only we would wake up
We'll see who really has seniority
#FACTS

Dear Mama

(Part 2)

Dear Mama

I miss you

I think about you everyday

And every morning I pray

That God has you in His arms and safe

Feeling no more pain

Suffering or sorrow

He said that He'll always be with us

But never promised tomorrow

This thing called life is deep

Whoever thought I would do all of this time

And have both you and Dad taken from me

I admit it really makes me sad

And even a little scared

To go back out in the world

And have you not there

To come home too

Eat ya cooking, laugh and just chill

Shit ain't fair sometimes

To the point that I can't believe it's real

Dear Mama,

I love you

I hope you hear my prayers

When I close my eyes

And listen to my heart

I can feel you near

This just aint fair

And at times the pain is a lil too much to bare

My world is different

Without you here

But I'm gonna hold my head

And stay strong like you taught me too

You once told me that seeing me strong

Give you strength

So I'm doing this for you!

Gotta Love Me

On my me ish

Gotta love me

Cuz I'm all I got

I thought I had real love

But dealing with you takes a lot

Changing faces

Changing places

Running in the races of life

Making the same mistakes twice

With empty promises of being the official wife

Love don't take all of that

Not when it's real

It just flows like a river

No matter how you feel

It never fades

So how are you gonna love me tomorrow

But hate me today

You so fake

Krazy and whack

You don't deserve me at all

So I'm taking my love back!

Faithful

Oh Lord you're so faithful

And sometimes I wonder why

Even when I fall short

You continue to lift me high

Above my foes

You set my feet upon a rock

Indeed you had Your angels watching over me

Even when I was on the block

Runnin, druggin, thuggin and buggin

You preserved my life

Although it wasn't you I was loving

Now here I am

Delivered from the things of the past

Yet, I still fall short

But your faithfulness has surely surpassed

All of the fake mundane love

Given through the years

From so call fam, lovers and even my peers

You hear my prayers

Count my tears

You've given me so much strength

And calmed my fears

Now as I sit here

Contemplating my life

Indeed my Lord

Has redeemed me from strife

Even so, sometimes the pain

Still cuts like a knife

Lord, I'm crying

And it hurt so bad

I want to be free

And make up for the past

To move forward

And live up to my potential

I thank you for Your Word

Which is very instrumental

To where I am going

And all I can do

I'm so anxious to walk it out

But I cannot do it without You

Lord, I need you

To make a way

To bring me out of prison

And see a better day

Outside of these walls of silence

Free from the negativity, hurt, pain and violence

But a life of liberty, prosperity, fruitfulness and peace

A life when I am finally free

Just to be me

Lord, I know you are faithful

And hear my prayers

So I praise You in advance

And thank You for being here

For I'm still blessed and highly favored

And baby, favor ain't fair

I just wanna say

Thank You Jesus

For bringing me out of here!

Amen.

Missin U

I miss u

I miss us

And what we had

I really try not to think about u

Cuz when I do I get sad

In so many ways

You really were my first

So many years together

And a couple separated

Yet, I still feel the hurt

Well, in a way the pain has faded

I'm more disappointed

That our love didn't make it

It's frustrating that we really are no more

I don't know what's going on

I haven't been here before

I miss u

I really do

And I dont want too

I don't wanna write this poem

I dont wanna write at all

I don't wanna think about you

I don't wanna try to call

I don't wanna give u my tears

Don't wanna wish I was there
Don't wanna see u again
Cuz if I do
Then pain will win
I don't wanna think about who you are with
Who is touching you
Or the what if's
I just dont wanna admit
That in my heart
It's us that I miss
Man, why do I feel like this?
I miss u

The Jungle

Adorned with fig leaves as my skirt
And coconut shells covering my breasts
Barefoot and sweaty
Surrounded by natures best
The birds squawk and the monkeys swing
An elephant triumphs
While bathing her young in the stream
Crocodiles play hide and seek
Stalking their prey
As the lioness hunts
To feed her cubs for the day
I am here
In the middle of nowhere
Yet somewhere
With only my instincts as my guide
Sweat beating my brow
And nowhere to hide
I'm vulnerable, scared and all alone
How did I get here?
I really don't know
All I want is to go back home
Take it back to the good ole days
With mama fussin
While frying fish fillets

Block parties, water balloons and that grape kool-aid

We drunk all day

Damn, I wish I could've stayed

But now here I am

In the belly of the beast

As I snap back to my reality

These black and orange stripes have cornered me

It's fierce eyes piercing into the core of my being

I am almost convinced

That she can hear my heart beating

Like a drum

In this African sun

The beat intensifies

And now I know I'm almost done

Jazzy for dinner

Bon appetit

"I can't go out like this

Not after I beat the streets"

This mystified creature

Sashays her way to me

Now face to face and eye to eye

I know if I blink she will do me

So I keep my eye on the tiger

Not losing my focus

"Im not afraid of you anymore"

Then BAM--- HOCUS POCUS

I release a roar

So loud and so deep

That the earth trembles under my feet

With fire in my eyes

I won't succumb to defeat

She graciously bows before me

In respect to the Queen that I am

My greatest challenge is now my triumph

As in the midst of the jungle I stand

I am in her territory

The sun beams accepting my glory

And this is me and the beast story

Epilogue

I'm in a place of solitude

As I bring these pages to an end

It's never good-bye or done with

A new chapter will begin

Whether it's in black and white

Or set in stone

Eventually my story will be told

Becuz it is my own

A diva with an old soul

Left in this cruel world alone

The Panther & Artists Love

Manifested in flesh and bone

Birthed with passion

And seasoned with pain

I hold my head

And continue to maintain

While being loved by few

Misunderstood by most

But respected by all

No matter where I am

I will always stand tall

Even when I fall

I get back up and continue to fight

No matter the adversary

In the darkest night

I wont blink twice

It's in my blood

It's in my spirit

It's in my heart

I give it freely

Only to be returned ripped apart

Regardless of what

I am me

Malii's babygirl

So you can picture me rollin

With my middle finger up

Screaming out

"FUCK DA WORLD"

About The Author

Da'Diva Jazz was raised in Newark, New Jersey. In 2017, she was blessed with a new beginning after serving seventeen years in the Department of Corrections (DOC). She currently resides in South Jersey where she lives a serene, productive life with her family.

She currently maintains two full-time jobs and has recently branched out into the world of urban poetry and literature, fashion and entrepreneurship. Da'Diva Jazz is a student at Rowan College where she majors in Human Services and slated to graduate with her bachelors degree in May 2019. She is a faithful member of Micah 7 Ministries in Piscataway, New Jersey. This is her first published work, and she is currently writing her second.